HEALING

A collection of poems

GABRIELLA ALZIARI

Illustrations by Marina Wino

To Pearl,
for all her wisdom

Author's Note

There is a tiger within me,
ferocious and raw

With my pen,
I hold him like a friend
and all my pain
flows into power

CONTENTS

My Solitude

Poetry

I will breathe life
into my poetry

It flickers within me,
a lit match,
ready to explode
into a bonfire

Excavation

My future pages lie inside me
like a copper wire

I grow the urge to know them.

My body is a cave,
words rest in every crevice

I nudge them from within.
They spread like peacock's wings,
a mystic fan of dreams

I am the archaeologist
of my womanhood.

Unearthing vulnerabilities,
I excavate myself.

Diamonds and dirt
rest side-by-side
like lovers,
never one
without the other

I sift through every year,
emptying the remnants

My power flows from patience.

My words,
they shine like gold

Embryo

I move on from my past
with all its flaws and fictions

I am too unafraid
to hide in stowaways.

Once there was a time
my sun was set to rise

It dampened like a candle,
under a cruel pretense.

At night I stretch my limbs,
remind myself I'm here

Find shelter in the shadows,
re-light my quivering pride

I tell myself,
let go

The embryo of me
slips gently from my body,
a stillborn fantasy

To me it was unfolding,
a ceaseless meditation

Gone is what once was,
but not what can
still be

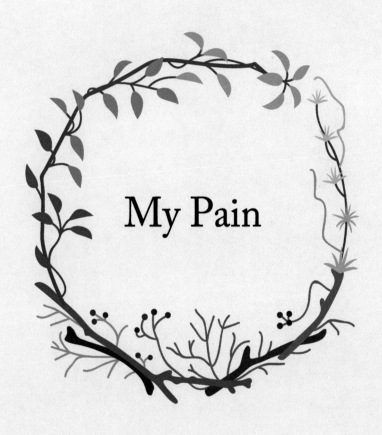

My Pain

Undressing

He unravels me like film,
licks the color from my skin
injects me with anemia,
inhaling as I tremble

Impalpable murmuring,
unfamiliar sweat.
I melt there like a snowflake,
sinking to the floor

My Bones

Stepping back into my life
to the recesses of my past,
I remember what was pure,
and feel what was terrible.

Crying in your arms,
losing myself in your heartbeat,
tracing my fingers through hundreds of days,
stacked like slides on a movie reel.

Tasting your affection,
sensing that you never knew me.
I became you,
but you only felt me.

I think how sad it is
that my worth
crumbled to nothing.

I shiver in the mist of memories.
I sew you into my bones.

War

You have an energy
like an animal
when you crawl into my cave
and forget that I am fragile,
human and torn

You are not light love.
You are the true trenches,
pure blood and grime,
the shrapnel that warns me,
rupturing alive
as I crawl, desperate for shelter

In the distance, I hear you
at war
and my candle only flickers

In the distance
you resist the showers,
bursts streaming down
like meteors, invincible

I reach deep within myself,
find my inner halo,
clasp my hands in the thick of night,
become drunk on staying alive

My internal flame burns scarlet
the sounds humming,
subdued
the war no longer mine

My Passion

Ghosts

Your kisses pepper me like freckles,
lining my face like pigment
You are deep in my crevices,
whispering soft as a rainstorm,
seductive as the wetness
dripping down my thighs

We are ghosts to one another.

But I become your vision
of the perfect woman,
and you become
the recipe
for my self-completion

Untaming

Let me drift
into a wave of nothingness
Let me slip
into your heat and fragile kisses
Let me sink
into your spirit,
embedding in
the barren parts of you

Let me explore
your secret depths
to find
your hidden crystals
Let me taste
your bitterness,
the sweet within the sour

Let me hold
the whole of you,
your softness shrouded
in ambition

You are my forest fire,
my comfort in the darkness.
My love for you is boundless:
an essence that cannot be tamed

Healing

I breathe into you
like a soft summer sunset,
caressing your failures, painting over your flaws,
the muscles and bones weaving together
as I plant tender flowers
on the bridge of your shoulder

And doesn't it burn
when I blossom within you,
as I smooth away scars
with my light and my love

We are delicate threads,
knit together as one

You breathe into me.
We heal one another.

My Power

Wild

I am a wild girl,
I will not be tamed.

You try to thread the needle
under my skin,
sew your ways into my flesh,
re-arrange my life so it reflects yours.

I will not follow your footsteps
like dominoes,
collapsing on top of each other
without breathing, without wanting
something more

More adventurous
than the blueprint you hunch over
alone in your room
after you've searched yourself
and mislaid who you are

I watch you through the window
you would never light a candle,
you would never honor the spark
that ignites within you
and reminds you
that you are
as wild
as me

Danger

There is a tremor stirring in me,
a roar as fierce as fire
it rises from within
and warms my tender core

A pure determination,
my will, as full as water,
I spread my arms and stand
at the precipice of danger

Nothing
is as brave
as the wilderness within me.
Nothing is as bold
as my own
flourishing

Meteor

In the shelter of twilight,
as shadows drape around us
I crumple
like a willow,
collapsing into you
I weep
like a cherry,
retreating to your core
finding refuge in its beat

I turn my pain to power
unfurl in your elixir,
my tender little heart
cracking open
like an agate

My inner essence flares
like a signal, like burnt sage,
the meteor in me
shining bright for the whole world

My Spirituality

Bath

At night I
lower my body towards
the bathwater

Wrinkle my fingers,
slip into weightlessness,
peel my skin
and spread my toes

In the silence, I shed
the weight
of my burdens

In the stillness, I embrace
the angel within me

Auric Fields

Let us talk:
softly,
covering the world in vibrations

Let us whisper:
intentionally,
our words inaudible to others

Let us kiss:
passionately,
at last, I am with you

Your lips,
the breath to my final meditation

Your embrace,
the aura guarding me from winter

Your spirit,
rushing through me,
all at once!

Let us fall
into an intoxicated love
so deep, that all else is quiet

So pure
that your aura
is mine

Sunlight

You are the sunlight
that seeps through the cracks
on my windowsill

You touch the hidden parts of me,
the secrets of my soul

You reach within my silence,
shedding light to
dispel darkness

The warmth of rays envelops me

You fill
my world
with dreams

The End

Acknowledgements

I deeply appreciate everyone who has supported my poetry.

A special thanks goes to my parents, brother, and extended family, who have always seen the light in me, even before I found it in myself.

My friends, who told me I would publish a book one day.

Pearl, who encouraged me and told me this was my future, regardless of how much or little money is in writing.

Marina, for bringing my words to life so magically.

Fida, for pushing me to put the right words in the right places.

My spirit guides and angels, because you are all very real, and it is because of you that this is possible.

Daniel, the inspiration for many of my poems, my spiritual partner and greatest love.

Thank you from the bottom of my heart. You have allowed me to achieve one of my life's longest dreams.

About the Author

Gabriella is a poet living in Washington, DC. She graduated with a Bachelor of Arts in English Literature from Kenyon College and a Master of Science in Organizational Behavior from the London School of Economics. She has been writing poetry since she was 14. Through her words, Gabriella hopes to spread a message of self-empowerment, showing her readers they are capable of anything as long as they practice self-love. Apart from writing, Gabriella loves making art, practicing mindfulness, and taking walks in nature.

You can see more of Gabriella's work by visiting her website, www.gabriellaalziari.com, and following her on Instagram @gabriellaalziari.

Made in the USA
Middletown, DE
01 March 2023

25988038R00029